Loud and Scary People

Written By Helen Tilford

Illustrated By Alexandra Gold

To my grandchildren,
and to my grandson, Anthony,
who helped make this book possible.

Loud and scary people are having a hard time with scary feelings inside of them.

They don't know it.
It's like a big dark room inside them,
that has many little places for
feelings to hide.

Oh oh--what's this behind the door?
Someone said a mean thing to me
and I felt sad.

What's hiding under that table?
Someone pushed me and I felt scared.

There's a big scary something
just by the chair.
Someone yelled at me in front of my
friends and I wanted to cry.

But all these scary feelings stay hidden
in the secret room of our hearts.
And there they grow into bigger and
Bigger and BIGGER scary feelings,
until they spill over and become words
and actions that can scare others.

When they scare others they don't feel the frightening places in the dark room of the hidden hurts!

What to do about ALL this fright?
Turn on the light in the dark room.
See that everyone has those same
scary feelings, and we all want them
to go away so we can feel brave
and not afraid.

Being brave is being kind
and will help you inside
to let all those scary sad,
and embarrassing places feel better
and feel more safe.
Be kind to others and the light
is turned on.

Be mean to others and the scary places
get darker and Darker and DARKER
and more frightening.

So please remember to stop being afraid of your own scary feelings, so you don't have try to SCARE ME!!!

Yours in light and love,

Helen Tilford